A Day in the Life: Polar Animals

Arctic Fox

Katie Marsico

Heinemann Library
Chicago, Illinois

www.capstonepub.com
Visit our website to find out more information about Heinemann-Raintree books.

To order:
☎ Phone 800-747-4992
💻 Visit www.capstonepub.com
to browse our catalog and order online.

Edited by Rebecca Rissman, Daniel Nunn, and Sian Smith
Designed by Joanna Hinton-Malivoire
Picture research by Hannah Taylor
Originated by Capstone Global Library Ltd

Library of Congress Cataloging-in-Publication Data

Marsico, Katie, 1980-
  Arctic fox / Katie Marsico.—1st ed.
    p. cm.—(A day in the life: polar animals)
  Includes bibliographical references and index.
  ISBN 978-1-4329-5329-4 (hc)
  ISBN 978-1-4329-5336-2 (pb)
  1. Arctic fox—Juvenile literature. I. Title.
  QL737.C22M36424 2012
  599.776'4—dc22   2010050012

Acknowledgments
We would like to thank the following for permission to reproduce photographs: agefotostock: Morales Morales, 6; Alamy: All Canda Photos, 15, 23, Arcticphoto, 8, 23, Dmitry Deshevykh, 10, 11, 23, Radius Images, 14, Rolf Nussbaumer Photography, 19, Terry Whittaker, 18, WILDLIFE GmbH, Cover; FLPA: Minden Pictures/Michio Hoshino, 5; Getty Images: Joe McDonald, 16, Richard Kemp, 17, Science Faction/Steven Kazlowski, 22; iStockphoto: tobiasjo, 23 (lemming); Nature Picture Library: Wild Wonders of Europe/de la Lez, 21; Shutterstock: ecoventurestravel, Back Cover, 20, 23, Incredible Arctic, 7, 9, Thomas Barrat, Back Cover, 13, Steven Kazlowski, 4, 23, Tom Brakefield, 12

The publisher would like to thank Michael Bright for his assistance in the preparation of this book.

Contents

Some words are shown in bold, **like this**.
You can find them in the glossary on page 23.

What Is an Arctic Fox?

An Arctic fox is a **mammal** that lives in snowy areas.

All mammals have some hair on their bodies and feed their babies milk.

Arctic foxes are about the size of small dogs.

The color of their fur helps them to **blend in** and hide.

What Does an Arctic Fox Look Like?

In the fall and winter, Arctic foxes have thick, white fur.

Their fur matches the color of the snow and keeps them warm.

In the spring and summer, Arctic foxes have gray or brown fur.

Arctic foxes also have a bushy tail and furry feet.

Where Do Arctic Foxes Live?

Arctic

Arctic foxes live in a part of the world called the **Arctic**.

In the Arctic it is light all day and all night for part of the summer.

In the Arctic it is dark all day and all night for part of the winter.

The Arctic is one of the coldest and windiest places on Earth!

What do Arctic Foxes do at Night?

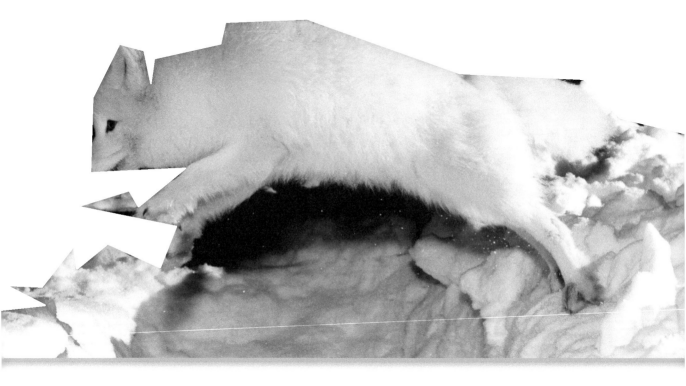

Arctic foxes are **nocturnal**.

This means they are usually more **active** at night.

Arctic foxes often spend part of the night hunting for food.

They have an excellent sense of smell that helps them to hunt in the dark.

hare

Arctic foxes mainly eat **lemmings**.

They also hunt voles, hares, and nesting birds.

Arctic foxes sometimes look for scraps left over by larger animals, such as polar bears.

Many dig holes in the ground where they bury food to eat later.

W--t H--..t ^r ti Foxes?

wolf

Polar bears and wolves hunt Arctic foxes.

Other types of foxes also attack and kill them.

People hunt Arctic foxes for their thick fur.

Arctic foxes sometimes escape their enemies by **blending in** with their surroundings.

Do Arctic Foxes Live in Groups?

Arctic foxes live alone from late fall to early spring.

They spend time in family groups for the rest of the year.

A group of Arctic foxes is called a skulk
or a leash.

These groups are usually made up of 2
or 3 adults, and 3 to 12 babies.

What Do Arctic Foxes Do in the Day?

Arctic foxes are usually less **active** during the day.

They might spend some of this time resting.

Arctic foxes go hunting when the animals they want to eat are awake.

If those animals are awake in the day, then Arctic foxes sometimes hunt during the day.

What Are Baby Arctic Foxes Like?

den

Baby Arctic foxes are called kits or pups and they are born inside **dens**.

Baby foxes look like small versions of their parents.

Kits start hunting when they are about 14 weeks old.

They soon learn how to survive outside the den in the frosty **Arctic**!

fur

tail

mouth

foot

 **active** busy doing lots of things

 **Arctic** area surrounding the North Pole. It is very cold in the Arctic.

 **blend in** to match the colors of the surroundings and be hard to see

 **den** hole in the ground where Arctic foxes sleep and give birth to their babies

 **lemming** small, mouse-like animal with a short tail

 **mammal** animal that feeds its babies milk. All mammals have some hair or fur on their bodies.

 **nocturnal** awake and active at night

Books

Person, Stephen. *Arctic Fox: Very Cool! (Uncommon Animals)*. New York City: Bearport Publishing, 2009.

Sisk, Maeve. *Arctic Foxes*. New York City: Gareth Stevens Publishing, 2010.

Websites

www.defenders.org/wildlife_and_habitat/wildlife/arctic_fox.php

Find out about the Arctic fox on the Defenders of Wildlife Website.

animals.nationalgeographic.com/animals/mammals/arctic-fox/

Learn more about the Arctic fox with National Geographic.

Index